FROM SMALL TOWN TO FOOTBALL STAR

ADAM THIELEN

by
Lindsay VonRuden
& Ryan Jacobson

Minneapolis, Minnesota

Dedication

This is dedicated to the entire Thielen family; to my parents, Brad and Mary; to my brothers, Dalton and Dawson; and to my classroom students of the past, present, and future. Thanks for your never-ending support and the joy you bring to my life daily. —Lindsay

Acknowledgments

Special thanks to everyone who contributed stories, information, and/or photographs—especially Peter and Jayne Thielen, Amanda Welken, Angela Escalante, and Caitlin Thielen for your help in filling in the details—as well as Paul Allan, Craig Caulfield, Janaye Johnson, and Robert Williams. We are thankful for the opportunity to share with the world how wonderful a person Adam is.

Proofread by Emily Beaumont
Cover design by Ryan Jacobson and germancreative

Adam Thielen photograph (front) by Bruce Kluckhohn. Copyright 2018 The Associated Press. Back image copyright Minnesota State Athletics. Used with permission. For additional photography credits, see page 111.

10 9 8 7 6 5 4 3 2

Copyright 2018 by Lindsay VonRuden and Ryan Jacobson
Published by Lake 7 Creative, LLC
Minneapolis, MN 55412
www.lake7creative.com

ISBN: 978-1-940647-32-6; eISBN: 978-1-940647-33-3

TABLE OF CONTENTS

PROLOGUE

The football was snapped. The Minnesota quarterback dropped back to pass. Standing on the Vikings' 36-yard line, he spotted his receiver's familiar purple jersey. His favorite target streaked down the right sideline.

With all of his might, the quarterback hurled the football deep down the field. The Dallas Cowboys defender tried to grab the speedy receiver, and the referee threw a penalty flag. But it didn't matter. The young Vikings star pulled in the football at Dallas's nine-yard line and battled forward into the end zone.

Randy Moss had just scored his second touchdown of the first quarter, giving Minnesota a 20–6 lead.

Inside his home, eight-year-old Adam Thielen jumped off the basement couch and cheered excitedly. He wanted to spike the football that he cradled in his arms, but his dad wouldn't like that. Instead, he gripped the laces in his small hands and tossed the ball a few feet into the air. He caught it and did his best to mimic the thrilling play he had just seen.

Adam loved watching football with his dad. Together, they talked about the plays, the players, and especially

Randy Moss. It was Moss's first year in the National Football League (NFL), but he was already Adam's favorite.

This game was especially memorable because it was Thanksgiving Day 1998. Moss caught 3 passes for 163 yards and 3 touchdowns, as well as a 2-point conversion. His performance spearheaded an impressive 46–36 win.

After the game, Adam did what he always did: He went outside and played catch, re-enacting all the best plays from the game he had just watched. In his imagination, he was Randy Moss, scorching the defense for touchdown after touchdown.

Like so many other boys, Adam dreamed of playing in the NFL. But that was just a dream. It couldn't possibly come true. Could it?

Max Disse and Adam dressed up for a school Halloween party.

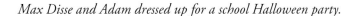

1

⟨⟨⟨⟨⟨ NEW NEIGHBORS ⟩⟩⟩⟩⟩

Adam John Thielen was born on August 22, 1990, at 4:15 a.m. in Detroit Lakes, Minnesota. His parents, Peter and Jayne Thielen, named Adam after his great-grandfather. *That* Adam Thielen had been a small-scale dairy and cattle farmer in the Detroit Lakes area. Peter was a salesman, selling buildings for Foltz Buildings. Jayne worked as a secretary at a Catholic school, and later as a stay-at-home mom, who kept active in the community. She ran area golf programs and was a member of the Detroit Lakes Athletic Foundation.

The newly born Adam was the youngest of three children. Peter and Jayne already had two daughters, Amanda and Angie.

The Thielen family was well known in their corner of northwestern Minnesota, probably because the family was so big. Adam's dad had five brothers and four sisters, which meant a lot of aunts, uncles, and cousins for Adam. Of course, Adam fit right in. He bore the Thielens' trademark brown hair and brown eyes, and he shared such family traits as a love for popcorn, an infectious laugh, and a competitive spirit.

If Adam's childhood could be described in one word, it would be "active." Adam was constantly outside, playing one sport or another. When he was four, his family moved into a house seven miles out of town. The huge yard was a perfect setting for whatever game struck his interest. The only real problem was that he didn't have many neighbors to play with.

Fortunately for Adam, the Johnson family lived just a quarter of a mile away—and they had two children looking for a playmate. Janaye was the same age as Adam, and Davis was a few years younger. The three of them spent so much time together that they actually wore a trail through the woods between each others' homes.

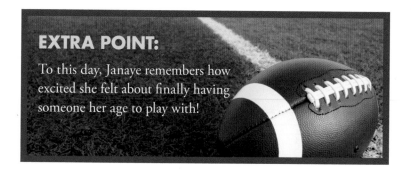

EXTRA POINT:

To this day, Janaye remembers how excited she felt about finally having someone her age to play with!

Adam was sports-focused even from a young age, and the Johnsons were always happy to join in the fun. If Adam wasn't out practicing layups at the basketball hoop, he was setting up cones to run his own football drills. He and Davis loved running routes and catching passes from Janaye. Adam almost always wore a tattered Minnesota

Vikings jersey. He loved to try tricky catches where he either dove for the ball or snagged it near the sideline while keeping his feet in bounds. Janaye threw so many make-believe touchdowns to Adam and Davis that she nicknamed herself their "permanent quarterback."

Adam dreamed of a career in the NFL. He always had fun with his friends, trying to mimic the great plays he saw on TV. But Adam took those backyard practices very seriously. He always worked hard and stayed focused. The skills he developed at home in his yard might one day serve him on a *real* football field.

For all the time that Adam spent with Janaye and Davis at home, he didn't see them at school. While the Johnson children attended public school, Adam was enrolled in a

Adam, Janaye, and Davis.

Catholic school. The experience helped Adam to develop strong religious beliefs, but the strict, rigid structure was not a perfect fit. Adam's class was small—just 20 students in the entire grade—and his mind often wandered to playing sports and going outside. He had a hard time sitting still, and he soon took on the role of "class clown." He loved goofing off to make his classmates laugh, which often got him into trouble.

Adam's teachers began sending home a notebook with him. In it, they would write about Adam's day. His parents would read it—and find out if he was being good. The next day, they would send it back to school with him, so the teachers could write in it again. In this manner, Mrs. Thielen kept in close contact with Adam's teachers, helping to keep him on task and his behavior in check. Despite these efforts, Adam still struggled in the classroom setting.

By the time Adam was nine years old, his mom and dad recognized that a change was needed. School was not going as well as they had hoped. Plus, Adam didn't get enough opportunities to feed his passion for sports. Mr. and Mrs. Thielen needed to do something for Adam. The question was . . . what?

2

⟪⟪⟪ FOURTH GRADE ⟫⟫⟫

The Catholic school had been an ideal setting for Adam's sisters, Amanda and Angie. But it wasn't right for Adam. When he reached the fourth grade, his parents made an important decision. They moved him from the private school into a public one: Roosevelt Elementary in Detroit Lakes. This new setting allowed "active Adam" more time to play and have fun—and more students to interact with!

At Roosevelt Elementary, Adam took full advantage of the wide open area next to the playground. It made for an excellent football field. No matter the season, no matter the conditions—rain, snow, wind, or mud—Adam wanted to play.

With an August birthday, he was one of the youngest students in the fourth grade. Even so, the other students all wanted him on their teams. For Adam, every game was a serious affair. He used each play to learn and become better at the sport. Yet he always wore a smile and made sure the games were fun.

Adam wasn't just a football fanatic. He went out for every sport he could, including two winter sports: basketball and wrestling. A basketball coach gave Adam some grief about that, telling him that he couldn't do both when he was older. So that winter, Adam chose just one. His father had been a wrestler in high school. His sisters were in basketball, so he had connections to both sports. Adam preferred basketball, so he made the decision to quit wrestling and stick with hoops.

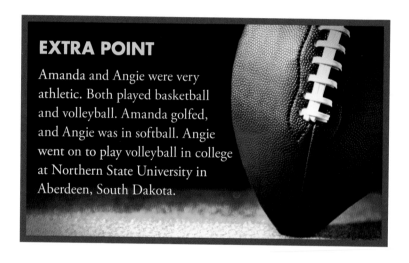

EXTRA POINT

Amanda and Angie were very athletic. Both played basketball and volleyball. Amanda golfed, and Angie was in softball. Angie went on to play volleyball in college at Northern State University in Aberdeen, South Dakota.

At home, Adam's love of sports shone through in his bedroom decor. His blanket and matching curtains were patterned with baseballs, basketballs, and footballs. His walls and shelves were adorned with Minnesota sports memorabilia. Adam's favorite decoration was a poster that featured three of his favorite Minnesota Vikings: Daunte Culpepper, Randy Moss, and Cris Carter.

Adam had a special reason for loving that poster. In 2003, family friend Clayton Borah invited Adam to join

Adam met Vikings quarterback Daunte Culpepper at training camp.

his family on a road trip to Vikings training camp. Adam rode with the Borahs to Mankato, Minnesota—six hours away—to watch a day of practice. Adam had been so excited that he hardly slept the night before.

Mr. Borah knew Culpepper, so Adam got to meet the young quarterback. It was a thrilling experience for Adam, but Moss was his favorite player. When Culpepper heard this, he waved at Moss and signaled for him to come over. But Moss just waved and walked away in a rush.

Culpepper didn't give up. He wanted to make the fan's day. A short while later, he tracked down Moss and got him to come over. Adam was able to meet his childhood hero and to get the receiver's autograph.

3

ᚱ SUMMER ᚱ

Vikings training camp wasn't the only thing Adam loved about summer. He participated in almost every sport offered—including baseball, basketball, and football. He also spent countless hours at a community education center called the Rec. It was a place for children to hang out together, playing games like kickball, dodgeball, and four square.

The building itself was tiny, just large enough to house sporting equipment, craft supplies, and a freezer full of frozen treats to help kids cool down on hot summer days. The staff at the Rec usually consisted of local high school and college students. It was open Monday through Friday, all summer long, and was free to visit. Along with popular sports, the Rec offered everything from crafts and board games to old-fashioned potato sack races and water balloon tosses.

Adam's mom ran the junior golf program at the local Lakeview Golf Course, and she liked to bring Adam with her. Sometimes, he sat and listened to golf lessons. Other times, he got to play.

If he wanted to golf, his mom made him ask other golfers to let him tag along. Usually, the golfers said, "yes,"

Adam loved to go tubing with cousins at Grandpa and Grandma's lake.

but sometimes they turned him down. Either way, it helped Adam develop social skills and get used to speaking with people of all ages. Plus, Adam learned a lot about golfing from the different people who played with him.

Summer in "Lakes Country" meant swimming. Adam was lucky enough to have grandparents who lived near a lake. A trip to Grandpa and Grandma Thielen's house meant tubing and riding on a Jet Ski, as well as playing in the yard with his sisters and cousins. If no one else wanted to play catch, Adam would ask a neighbor to throw the football around with him.

Adam did sit down and relax once in a while—to watch sports when he needed a break from playing them! He enjoyed cheering on the Minnesota Timberwolves, Twins, and Vikings. Most of his favorite movies were about sports, too. He watched *Air Bud*, *Angels in the Outfield*, and *Little Giants* over and over again.

Adam attended local sporting events—but not to watch. He gathered whichever students he could find and seized the opportunity to play. At the high school football field, Adam starred in his own games of football. At high school basketball games, he could often be found in the hallways, playing tag.

Even after Adam graduated from elementary school, his love of sports never faded. In fact, in middle school, it only grew stronger.

4

᚜᚜᚜ MIDDLE SCHOOL ᚜᚜᚜

Adam continued to take part in all of his favorite sports. During the fall season, he played football. In winter, it was basketball. When spring arrived, Adam found time for baseball and golf.

His mother knew that Adam focused more on sports than he did on school. Because of this, he sometimes struggled with his homework. But the family rule was that the kids had to maintain good grades, or they wouldn't be allowed to play sports. Because his parents took this rule very seriously, so did Adam. He worked as hard in the classroom as he did in practice—and it paid off. Adam never missed a game due to bad grades.

As Adam continued to grow, he was better able to compete with his family members. He often played basketball against his dad. Their favorite game together was HORSE, a simple contest in which each player tried to make baskets that the other would miss.

When Dad wasn't available, Adam played hoops with Angie. Both loved to tease the other. Adam especially enjoyed referring to himself as "money" when he was winning. Adam and Angie played catch together, too. Adam got angry with himself whenever he dropped a ball.

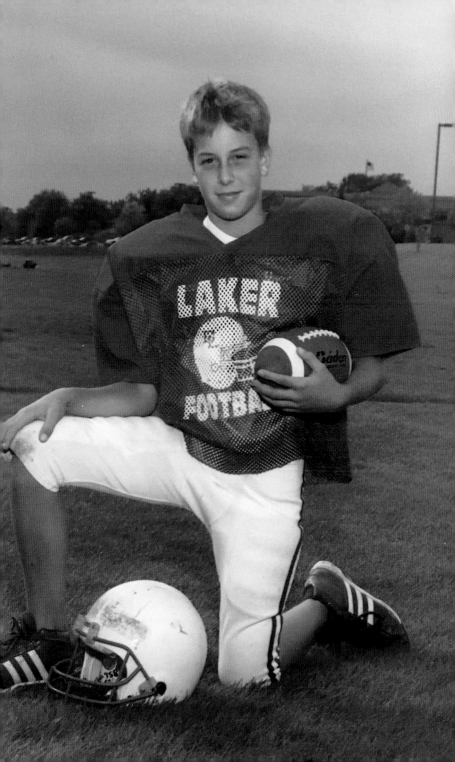

Eventually, the countless hours of playing at home began to fade. Sports practices took up much of Adam's time. Instead of having fun with Janaye and Davis after school, Adam worked on improving his skills with teammates and coaches.

The seasons came and went. Adam shuffled from practice to practice, from summer camp to summer camp, from game to game. The family still lived seven miles out of town. So time spent in the car began to add up—both for Adam and his mom, who usually delivered him wherever he needed to go.

When Adam was 14 years old, his family decided to move into town. This would make Adam's sports schedule easier on everyone. The Thielens found a home in the neighborhood where Adam's best friend, Josh Herzog, lived. Now, practices were just a walk, a bike ride, or a short drive away.

The move into town didn't bring Adam much closer to the Twin Cities, though. His family was more than three hours away. Nevertheless, Adam seized any opportunity to attend professional sporting events. One of his favorite stars was Minnesota Timberwolves basketball legend Kevin Garnett.

He may have been a sports fanatic, but Adam was still a Minnesota boy, through and through. He found time to enjoy the most beloved of Minnesota traditions. Adam and his father spent many hours fishing, hunting, snowmobiling, four-wheeling, and snowboarding.

In school, Adam found a role model in Bob Gorden, his basketball and golf coach. Gorden inspired Adam and helped him learn to improve as an individual and as a team player. The coach was especially helpful in bettering Adam's golf game.

Golf was not always easy for Adam. While his family loved to play, the sport frustrated him. There were times when he smacked around his golf clubs or threw golf balls in anger. Coach Gorden helped Adam to become more patient, and Adam's love of the game soared. By the eighth grade, Adam was on the junior varsity golf team.

He was becoming a better athlete in middle school. But high school awaited. How would he fare against a school full of students who were weeks, months, and years older than he was?

Adam and his friend Kyle Fode attended a Timberwolves game in 2003.

5

⟨⟨⟨⟨⟨ JUNIOR VARSITY ⟩⟩⟩⟩⟩

In September of 2004, Adam began attending Detroit Lakes High School. There, he realized that being young for his grade was not to his advantage. Everyone else got driving permits and began learning to drive. Adam wasn't old enough.

Even worse, when it came to sports, Adam wasn't as tall or as strong as his classmates. He was a small, skinny, 14-year-old boy. That was bad news for Adam—but it was also good news. To compete against others, he had to put forth extra effort. He had to work harder and longer than anyone else. Even that wasn't always enough. Sometimes, he struggled. But this was a good struggle, and Adam learned a lot about perseverance. No matter how badly things went, he never quit. He kept on doing his best, every day.

Adam's football season was quiet. He played junior varsity, but he was too small for varsity. Still, he got to put on his football gear and join the team on Friday nights. Standing on Mollberg Field, under the bright lights, Adam felt like a real athlete. The stands only held around 400 people, but Adam loved being there with family, friends, and hometown fans cheering.

Off the field, Adam found that ninth grade meant more homework than ever before. Balancing schoolwork and sports was not easy, but he knew that he had to do it. This was especially tricky when Adam was assigned novels to study. He procrastinated reading the books until the last possible moment. Sometimes, he waited too long. In those instances, he would read as much as he could right up until the test began.

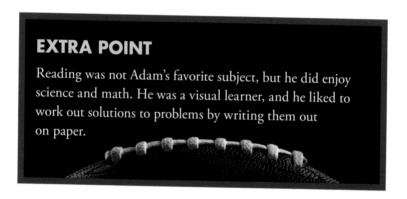

EXTRA POINT

Reading was not Adam's favorite subject, but he did enjoy science and math. He was a visual learner, and he liked to work out solutions to problems by writing them out on paper.

When basketball season came, Adam was on the junior varsity team. Most of the players he went up against were taller than him, but Adam still found ways to succeed. His goal was always to get rebounds and to make baskets.

By April, basketball was over and golf had begun. Adam made the varsity team, along with his best friend, Josh Herzog. Coaching the team was Bob Gorden, the same coach Adam had in middle school. The team golfed well together, and the players improved every week. In a year or two, that team would be tough to beat.

6

⟨⟨⟨⟨ **BASKETBALL STARTER** ⟩⟩⟩⟩

The following year didn't change much for Adam on the football field. He rarely played in the varsity games. Basketball, however, was a different story. The Laker team did not have many seniors, so some of the younger players got plenty of playing time—especially Adam.

He wasn't just good enough to play. He was in the starting lineup. Adam was a guard, and he took advantage of the chance to improve his skills against a higher level of competition. He was much younger than the players he went against, but Adam led the team in scoring with 16.5 points per game.

Unfortunately, the young team wasn't ready for the older and more experienced teams they faced. The Lakers finished with a record of 9–16. Still, Adam's efforts were rewarded when he was named to the all-conference team.

Adam also received an award in golf that spring. His team named him the "Most Improved Golfer." He wasn't yet one of the top golfers, but he continued to practice and get better.

During autumn of 2006, the high school junior improved enough on the football field to see his playing time increase—at wide receiver and defensive back. The team didn't throw the ball much, but when they did, Adam was usually the target. He finished the season with 25 catches for 435 yards and 4 touchdowns—about half of the Lakers' totals in every category. He helped Detroit Lakes to a respectable 7–3 record.

In basketball, Adam continued to perform well. He scored 13.6 points per game, and he hit an impressive 44 three-pointers throughout the year. He was tenacious and aggressive on the court—so much so that his parents worried he might accidentally hurt someone.

Mrs. Thielen felt so concerned that she spoke with Adam's coach, Wade Johnson. "Do you think you could tell him to settle down out there?" she asked.

Coach Johnson smiled and shook his head. "I will never tell a kid to be less aggressive. It's what makes him such a great player."

The coach was right. Adam gave his full effort every moment on the court, but he always remained in control. He continued playing hard, gritty basketball, and no one was ever hurt because of it. Still, Adam and the Lakers struggled to find wins. They finished the season 8–17.

The basketball starter could not crack the varsity baseball team, though. Adam played junior varsity—and batted ninth. But he continued to work. Adam's favorite sport was always whichever one he was playing, and he wanted to be as good as he possibly could. He wanted to make the varsity team.

When the coach finally moved him up, Adam showed what he could do. He had two hits, and he drove in two runs for the Lakers.

Not every game proved to be as successful. In one at bat, Adam smashed the ball deep into the outfield of Detroit Lakes' Washington Ballpark. Adam immediately knew that it was the hardest hit of his life. The baseball soared over the fence—home run!

Adam was so excited that he sprinted around the bases as fast as he could. After he touched home plate, he jumped and laughed and celebrated with his teammates . . . until the umpire called him out!

Adam had run so quickly around the bases that he missed first base. He never touched it. Now, his home run didn't count.

Despite this incident, Adam became a solid player. He was speedy, a great left fielder, and a good batter.

Summer came, and emotions ran high. Adam would have just one more year at Detroit Lakes High School— one more season of the sports he loved.

7

CROWN TOUCHDOWN CATCHES

Every year, the football team's goal was to reach the Minnesota State High School League championship game. It was played at the Hubert H. Humphrey Metrodome in Minneapolis. So, every year, a photograph of the Metrodome was placed in each player's locker. This served as a daily reminder of how far the team wanted to go. For Adam's senior year, the team was good enough to make it. But would they?

Head Coach Flint Motschenbacher put the kids to work, and that hard work paid off. The Lakers' offense started fast and never slowed. On the second play of the season, Adam sparked the team with a 39-yard reception versus Melrose. It set up a Lakers touchdown, and the rout was on. Adam added a thrilling 74-yard touchdown catch later in the game, giving Detroit Lakes a 47–20 victory.

Game after game, the Lakers brought home wins. Adam caught passes here and there—usually explosive deep plays—but he was mostly utilized as a tremendous blocker. He helped Detroit Lakes run away with the season. In their final regular-season game, the Lakers dominated Duluth–Central to finish with a record of 8–0

and the 2007 North Country Conference Championship. That was good enough to earn them a number-one seed in the playoffs.

They defeated ROCORI, 35–20, in their first playoff game. Then, on November 8, they squared off against Sartell–St. Stephen in the Section 8-4A championship.

The Lakers had early opportunities, and Adam found openings in the defense. But the passes fell incomplete, and those missed chances seemed to deflate the Detroit Lakes players. The Lakers were trounced, 35–8, and the dream season ended. It was a difficult loss for the whole community, who held such high hopes for the season. Adam was disappointed, as well. He had failed to make it to the Metrodome.

Despite the heartbreaking finish, Adam enjoyed a great deal of success. He tallied 20 catches on the season for 535 yards (an impressive 26.8 yards per catch) and 7 touchdowns. He was nicknamed "Adam 'All He Does Is Catch Touchdowns' Thielen" and "Motschenbacher's Most Dangerous Weapon" by a local sports writer. And Adam was named to the all-conference and all-state football teams.

Not surprisingly, Adam attracted attention from a couple of colleges. The University of Minnesota—Duluth tried to recruit him. But when their head coach moved away, Adam lost the offer. Minnesota State University—Mankato also showed some interest. But their coach moved, too, and Adam was again left empty-handed.

The senior took it upon himself to try and find a team that wanted him. He toured the campuses of multiple colleges—especially midsized colleges with strong football programs, like the University of North Dakota. Yet the coaches who talked to him all seemed to agree: Adam was too short, too skinny, and too slow. He was told more than once, "Stick to basketball."

Perhaps they were right. Adam wanted to play sports in college. If basketball gave him the best chance, then he would look for a team that would take him. But, first, he had one more season of high school hoops to play.

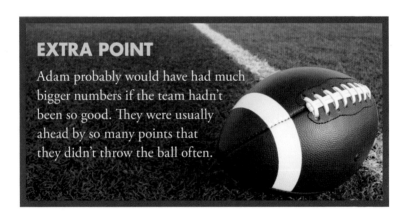

EXTRA POINT

Adam probably would have had much bigger numbers if the team hadn't been so good. They were usually ahead by so many points that they didn't throw the ball often.

8

~~~~~ SCHOOL RECORDS ~~~~~

Adam's final basketball season began with a new head coach, Robb Flint. The coach pushed the players like he would for a college team.

At first, the approach didn't seem to work. The Lakers started the season with 3 wins and 13 losses. Their first win came in mid-December. Adam and the Lakers battled to a 70–70 tie against the Alexandria Cardinals with just a few seconds to play.

Coach Flint put the ball in Adam's hands and let him go to work. The star player dribbled hard to the basket and put the ball up . . . and in! The referee blew his whistle. Adam was fouled on the play. He added a free throw, bringing his point total to 27 on the night and giving his Lakers the edge, 73–70.

A month later, on January 19, 2008, Adam's parents and sisters gathered in Little Falls, Minnesota, for what had the makings of a very special moment. Sure enough, Adam scored a basket in the second half that caused the crowd to go crazy with excitement. It was the 1,000th point of Adam's basketball career. He became only the second Laker ever to reach such an impressive milestone.

Adam's senior picture showed off his sports prowess.

Adam scored 12 points in the game, but his team fell, 58–45. In typical fashion, Adam didn't take much time to congratulate himself. Instead, he thought about what he did and did not do well—and how he could improve for the next game.

By the end of February, the Lakers found themselves with a disappointing record of 6–15. Loss number 16 looked imminent, as Adam's team traveled to Perham to take on the 18–3 Yellowjackets. No one expected the Lakers to win, not even their coach. He just hoped the boys would play hard and never give up.

Adam wasn't about to simply accept another loss. Instead, he played one of the best games of his high school career. He had something to prove—and prove it he did. He scored 11 of his team's first 13 points—and that eleventh point made Adam the all-time leading scorer in Detroit Lakes history!

But he wasn't done. Adam sank shot after shot; the Yellowjackets could not defend him. All told, Adam racked up 38 points, leading the Lakers to a stunning 66–57 victory.

The upset was part of a streak in which everything finally clicked on the court for the Lakers. The team finished strong, winning seven of its last nine games, giving them a record of 10–16 on the season. Adam averaged an amazing 22.2 points per game.

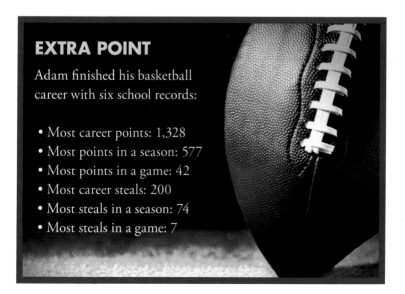

EXTRA POINT

Adam finished his basketball career with six school records:

- Most career points: 1,328
- Most points in a season: 577
- Most points in a game: 42
- Most career steals: 200
- Most steals in a season: 74
- Most steals in a game: 7

Despite Adam's success on the field and on the court, his greatest victory came on the golf course.

On Friday, June 6, the Detroit Lakes golfers found themselves trailing Orono by 13 strokes in the Class 2A state tournament. The Lakers had been ranked number one for most of the season, but it looked like they were about to blow their chance at a state title.

The players themselves didn't have much hope left. All they could do was go out on the Jordan, Minnesota, course and play as well as they were able. When the day was done and the scores were tallied, the impossible had happened. The Lakers had caught up with Orono—the schools were tied. Together, Detroit Lakes and Orono were crowned co-champions, and Detroit Lakes took home its first ever golf state championship!

Afterward, Adam turned to his teammates and said, "All right boys, we're jumping in the pond."

They did! Ever since then, the Detroit Lakes boys and girls teams jump into the pond to celebrate a golf championship. Adam started that tradition in 2008.

The state title was a fitting end to Adam's high school career. He knew that he owed a lot of his success to his parents and sisters. Their support was something that he would appreciate and cherish for the rest of his life. Now, he just hoped that his playing days weren't over.

9

⪡⪡⪡⪡ CHOOSING A COLLEGE ⪢⪢⪢⪢

As May of 2008 came to a close, Adam stood in his cap and gown for the high school graduation ceremony. He said goodbye to the classrooms where he spent countless hours learning—and to the courts and fields where he spent countless hours practicing.

He graduated with plenty of wonderful sports memories, but he wanted to make more of them. He wanted to play ball in college, but he didn't yet have a plan. He still wasn't sure if any college teams even wanted him.

Adam paused for pictures ahead of his graduation ceremony.

Adam spent much of that summer playing golf and baseball, and working at Herzog Roofing. He needed to save as much money as he could before starting college. Of course, he also needed to decide where to go.

A private school in Moorhead, Minnesota, contacted Adam in mid-June. Concordia College was just 50 miles from home. A coach invited Adam to join their basketball team, and Adam could likely play football, too. Concordia was an excellent college, but it was also expensive.

Adam could not pass up the opportunity to continue his sports career. He enrolled in the school, even though it would be difficult to pay the tuition. He hoped that he would get a good enough student loan to cover the costs.

The end of June brought another honor for Adam. He played in the 35th Annual Minnesota High School All-Star Football Game. The contest, held on June 28, featured the state's 85 best players and coaches from the 2007 season. Players were divided into Metro versus Outstate. Adam was selected to the Outstate team, and his coach was Flint Motschenbacher—Adam's high school coach.

The all-stars practiced for a week prior to the game, which was held in Saint Cloud, Minnesota. During that week, Adam caught the eye of Minnesota State University (MSU) in Mankato.

The game came and went. Adam's Outstate team fell to the Metro, 22–17, and Adam's only catch—a touchdown—was ruled out of bounds. But the game was a win for Adam. He just didn't know it yet.

Days later, he received a phone call from MSU's head football coach, Todd Hoffner. It was a short conversation. "We've got a $500 scholarship for you. Come play football in Mankato."

An instant thrill rose within Adam, mixed with a bit of surprise. He didn't know scholarships that small existed. But it was the only offer he had received. In truth, Adam wanted to play basketball more than football. But which was better for him: basketball at a Division III school or football at a larger Division II school?

Adam didn't hesitate. "Yep, I'm in. Let's do this."

Even though the scholarship was small, it felt good to know that a team wanted him enough to make an offer.

This change in plans had a dramatic effect on the rest of Adam's summer. Not only was he switching to a college at the other end of the state, he only had two weeks before MSU's freshman football camp would begin.

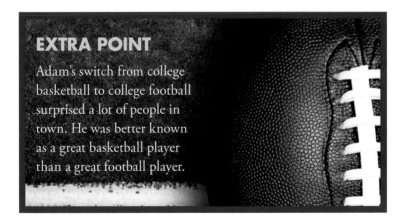

EXTRA POINT

Adam's switch from college basketball to college football surprised a lot of people in town. He was better known as a great basketball player than a great football player.

10

⟨⟨⟨⟨⟨ REDSHIRT FRESHMAN ⟩⟩⟩⟩⟩

Adam was still only 17 years old when he packed his college things into the family's light-blue Toyota Highlander. His clothes, Playstation 2, football spikes, beloved down comforter, and much more made their way into the vehicle. The Highlander was full by the time Adam finished.

His parents drove him to Mankato during the last week of July. They helped him set up his small dorm room, so he was ready for freshman football camp. For Mr. and Mrs. Thielen, this was goodbye to their last-born child. The house would be quiet without Adam. But seeing how excited he felt when they dropped him off, they knew he would be just fine. Then his parents said their emotional goodbyes and left. For the very first time, Adam was living on his own.

He went through a range of emotions. He missed his family and friends and the familiar comfort of Detroit Lakes. But at the same time, he was proud of himself for being there. He was independent now, able to begin carving out his own life. And although he didn't get the big scholarship of his dreams, he would be playing college football. Adam was grateful for that. Plus, he felt so excited to meet his teammates and begin a new football season that he could hardly contain himself. He actually had trouble sleeping.

College football was a lot different from high school. For one thing, the athletes were much bigger, stronger, and faster than Adam had ever been around before. Compared to them, Adam was too small—he weighed just 150 pounds.

The MSU coaches decided that Adam needed weight training to put on some muscle. They believed that he would be a valuable member of the team, but they wanted to make sure he was ready. So they decided to "redshirt" him for his freshman year.

Athletes were allowed to play college football for four years. "Redshirting" a player meant that he could practice with the team but couldn't play in any games. A "redshirt" year didn't count against the player's four years of college eligibility. Adam was able to grow and learn during the 2008 season, and he still had four more years to play!

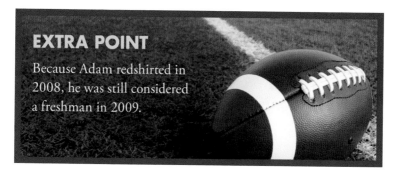

EXTRA POINT

Because Adam redshirted in 2008, he was still considered a freshman in 2009.

Adam with his nephew Ethan at a game.

The season and the school year seemed to pass in a blur. Adam didn't have his own car. So his parents drove six hours to get him every time he needed to go home—mostly just for holidays. His parents didn't mind at all. Family always came first for the Thielens, and the long drive was worth every moment spent with their son—even during harsh winter weather.

The following summer, Adam returned to Detroit Lakes. College had already taught him many lessons. He learned to appreciate his mom for doing laundry all of those years. He figured out that studying took a lot more time than taking tests. Adam also learned that hours spent in the weight room paid off. He looked and felt better than ever. He was truly ready to play college football.

At the end of July, Adam once again went back to Mankato for freshman football camp. He was determined to earn his way onto the field. And he did just that.

MSU Mavericks' fans got their first glimpse of Adam in his purple #9 jersey. Adam played in 9 of the team's 12 games. On the season, he caught 21 passes for 252 yards, including his first collegiate touchdown. Better yet, he helped his team finish with a 10–2 record and the Northern Sun Intercollegiate Conference (NSIC) South Division championship!

The season had been a good start for Adam, but it was only the beginning. No one could guess how much fans would grow to adore him.

11

ᚱᚱᚱᚱᚱ CAITLIN GRABOSKI ᚱᚱᚱᚱᚱ

Football was going well for Adam. Life off the field, however, was not quite as planned. Adam had plenty of friends . . . but no girlfriend.

Brittany, a local soccer player whom Adam knew, had an idea about that. Her friend, Caitlin Graboski, played soccer at Iowa State—and was also single. Brittany thought that Caitlin would be a good match for Adam.

That summer, Brittany introduced them on a video call. Adam was smitten, but Caitlin wasn't so sure. After all, they attended college nearly 200 miles apart. When Adam asked her out, Caitlin said, "No, thanks." She did agree to keep in touch with him. They regularly communicated on Facebook, and they texted back and forth, too.

For his sophomore football season, Adam bulked up to a muscular 182 pounds. It made a dramatic difference in his play. He quickly became regarded as one of the Mavericks' top offensive weapons.

On September 11, 2010, Adam showed what he could do. He powered an MSU victory over Northern State by catching 4 passes for 96 yards and 2 touchdowns. His 71-yard catch-and-run capped the scoring and gave his team a 21–14 victory.

Adam's family often came to his games to support him.

Overall, the season was an up-and-down affair. For a team with high hopes, the Mavericks finished a disappointing 6–5. But Adam had a breakout year. He was the team's leading receiver with 41 catches for 686 yards and 6 touchdowns. He gained a reputation for making amazing catches and for eating up yards after the catch. Adam was named MSU's Offensive Player of the Year. He was also awarded all-conference honors, earning a spot on the NSIC South Division Second Team Offense.

With football over, Adam spent the rest of his sophomore year studying and training—and keeping in touch with Caitlin. Adam was still interested in dating her, but Caitlin wouldn't give in.

Still, that summer, the two of them finally decided to meet in person. They took turns visiting one another, and they truly enjoyed each other's company. But they lived too far apart. Adam and Caitlin decided to go their separate ways. Their friendship soon faded, and the two of them fell out of touch.

That left Adam to concentrate on football. During the 2011 season, the junior wideout started in all 12 games for the Mavericks. He put together another impressive year. It was highlighted by a 45–23 victory against Wayne State, in which Adam caught 7 passes for 108 yards and a touchdown.

By the time the season ended, Adam tallied 62 receptions for 715 yards and 5 touchdowns. He also scored a touchdown on a kick return. Once again, Adam was named to the NSIC South Division Second Team Offense.

With just one more season to play, Adam planned to make his senior year a memorable one. He had no idea of the surprise that awaited him—one that would change his life forever.

12

⟨⟨⟨⟨⟨ DREAM SEASON ⟩⟩⟩⟩⟩

As far as Adam knew, the 2012 football season would be his last ever. In true Thielen fashion, he gave it his all. He wanted to see his team crowned as champions.

He had already established himself as a dangerous offensive weapon. But not only was he an incredible wide receiver, he also made plays as MSU's kick returner and punt returner. On top of that, Adam was so well respected that he was chosen as a team captain.

Adam remained focused on football, giving it his complete attention. But a familiar face from the past changed that—and became a very welcome distraction.

Caitlin Graboski transferred to Mankato to play soccer for the Mavericks. Adam's feelings for her came rushing back. The distance between them was gone. There were no more excuses. Adam asked Caitlin out, and she accepted.

He took her to a restaurant called Tav on the Ave. It was the first date of many. They began going everywhere together: sporting events, movies, bowling. Later, they even began a special tradition. During Christmas, they always went ice-skating at Rice Park in Saint Paul. With Adam in football and Caitlin in soccer, the two quickly became one of MSU's best known couples.

With Caitlin bringing balance—and a new joy—to Adam's life, the star wide receiver and his football team soared. The Mavericks went undefeated in the regular season, en route to a conference championship. Adam's year included his best collegiate performance: Against Southwest Minnesota State on October 13, he hauled in 11 catches for 167 yards. That included a touchdown catch with just 0:39 left on the clock. The dramatic eight-yard score tied the game at 24–24 and set up the Mavericks for a 34–31 victory in overtime!

In the playoffs, Adam's team won its first two games and advanced to the NCAA Division II Football Championship Semifinal. MSU squared off against the Valdosta State Blazers, and Adam helped his team get off to a hot start. His 17-yard touchdown catch early in the second quarter gave MSU a 10–0 lead.

But the Blazers reeled off three straight touchdowns. The Mavericks fought valiantly, but they could never close the gap. They eventually fell, 35–19, and Adam's career came to an end. He gave it his all in that final contest, with a game-high 128 yards receiving on 6 catches.

The Mavericks finished 2012 with a 13–1 record. Adam led the team in receiving with 74 catches for 1,176 yards and 8 touchdowns. He was named to the South Division's All-NSIC First Team.

Adam had every right to brag . . . at least, a little. But that wasn't his style. He remained humble about his success and rarely talked about it—even when people asked him.

When Adam did discuss football, it was usually to list all the ways he felt that he needed to get better.

Now that his college career was at an end, Adam had time to reflect upon all the support he had received, from beginning to end. Over the years, his family made the long, six-hour drive countless times to visit him and to watch him play. Even friends of the family would sometimes come from Detroit Lakes for a game.

Adam especially enjoyed visits from his sister Amanda and her son, Ethan. The young boy always wore an oversized Mavericks jersey with a nameplate on the back that read "Uncle Adam." That tradition continued when Amanda's second child, Zander, was born. He was there for Adam's final game at just three weeks old.

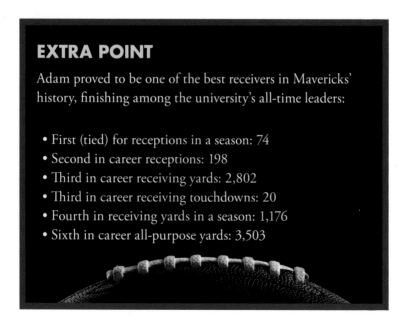

EXTRA POINT

Adam proved to be one of the best receivers in Mavericks' history, finishing among the university's all-time leaders:

- First (tied) for receptions in a season: 74
- Second in career receptions: 198
- Third in career receiving yards: 2,802
- Third in career receiving touchdowns: 20
- Fourth in receiving yards in a season: 1,176
- Sixth in career all-purpose yards: 3,503

13

⟨⟨⟨⟨⟨ CHASING A DREAM ⟩⟩⟩⟩⟩

Football had been an important part of Adam's life since he was five years old. He didn't feel ready to let it go. For a time, Adam thought about moving to Germany to play football there—or try the Canadian Football League or even Arena Football. But he set an even bigger goal.

A few days after his final college game, he told Caitlin, "I want to try and make it into the NFL."

She responded with a sideways look, one that might have suggested he had temporarily lost his mind. "Are you sure you don't want to get a normal job?" she offered.

Her response neither hurt nor offended Adam. She was trying to be supportive by keeping him focused on realistic goals. Making it in the NFL was a long shot.

According to the NCAA, 16,000 college football players were old enough for the NFL each year, but only around 250 were drafted. That included players from large, nationally known colleges like Alabama, Ohio State, and Notre Dame. Adam was attending a small university, which most of the country had never heard of. So his chances were very close to zero.

It was only December, though. Graduation was still five months away. Adam decided that he could do both. He would train hard for the NFL, and he would also pursue "regular" jobs as a backup plan.

"What's the worst that could happen?" he said. "So what if I don't make it? At least I can look back and know that I gave it my best shot. I'd be able to live with that."

Caitlin agreed that Adam's plan made sense. She offered him her full support.

Adam went to work, training with a former college teammate, Tommy Langford. Adam exercised tirelessly, knowing that he needed to be in the best shape of his life.

Adam and Caitlin at the Mavericks' soccer field.

But his physical condition was only part of the answer. Adam also needed to find a way to get noticed by the NFL teams.

Most of the top college players were invited to a special event in Indianapolis, Indiana, called the NFL Scouting Combine. Here, scouts from every professional football team watched and studied the players as they performed various tests and challenges. This helped the scouts decide which athletes would be best for their teams. Adam was not invited; he would need to find another way to get the teams' attention.

In his research, he discovered that there were smaller regional combines across the country during the month of March. Unknown players—including those from smaller schools—could attend these combines and show off their skills. Unfortunately, these smaller combines came with a price tag. Adam was welcome to participate in the regional combine in Chicago, Illinois, but he had to pay for it.

He didn't have enough money, so he borrowed $275 from his dad for the event, along with some extra money for gasoline, food, and a hotel room. Then he made the seven-hour drive to the Windy City, with Tommy and another friend.

The regional combine was different from the big one in Indianapolis. No scouts were present. Instead, players performed the drills, and their scores were recorded. These scores helped to show how strong, fast, and skilled each player was. The scores were sent to all 32 NFL teams.

Based on those scores, some players were selected to attend a super regional combine—with real NFL scouts.

Adam knew that he caught the football well and ran good routes. His chances depended almost entirely on how fast he was in the 40-yard dash. If he finished slower than 4.5 seconds, his dream would end. But if his time were faster than 4.5 seconds, there would still be hope.

Adam ran the race as quickly as he could. But no one told him his time. Instead, when the combine ended, he was given a website to look up on his laptop. The results would be posted there within the next several hours.

Adam and his friends celebrated the end of the combine with a delicious Chicago-style, deep-dish pizza. It was Adam's first big meal since he began training back in December.

After that, all Adam could do was wait.

14

⟨⟨⟨⟨⟨ FAST ENOUGH ⟩⟩⟩⟩⟩

Adam and his friends returned to their hotel room, where Adam could hardly contain his excitement. While the others relaxed and watched television, Adam sat at a desk all night, staring at the combine's website on his computer screen. The site remained blank, but Adam clicked the refresh button every few minutes, hoping the results would appear.

Click . . . click . . . click . . .

Adam didn't take his finger off the button for several hours.

Click . . .

Suddenly, the screen filled with new information! Adam sat up in his chair. His friends rushed over and stood behind him. Together, they scanned the screen, searching for his time in the 40-yard dash.

There it was: 4.45 seconds.

Adam leapt out of his chair. He hollered in excitement. His friends joined in, and high-fives started flying. The trio celebrated for a moment, but Adam immediately thought of Caitlin. He called her and shared the news.

As it turned out, Adam was right. His time was good enough to get him an invitation to the super regional combine in Dallas on April 7 and 8. Once more, Adam borrowed money from his dad to pay for travel expenses. But this time, his dad came along. Mr. Thielen even talked some people into letting him into the stadium to watch.

EXTRA POINT

The difference between 4.45 seconds and 4.5 seconds is 0.05 seconds. That's three times faster than the time it takes to blink!

Adam again performed well at the combine. A few scouts pulled him aside and talked to him. Still, nothing was guaranteed. There were a lot of great players looking for spots with just 32 NFL teams.

The 2013 NFL draft took place from April 25 to April 27. For seven rounds, each team had an opportunity to choose one former college player for their team. Some teams also received bonus picks. All together, 254 players were chosen.

Adam was not one of them. No team believed in him enough to use a precious draft pick on him. This was not a surprise, though. Adam didn't imagine that his name would be called during the three-day event. In fact, Adam didn't even watch the draft. He spent the weekend with his family. At one point, they went mini-golfing.

His hopes rested on what came after the draft. College students who weren't picked by a professional team became "free agents." They were welcome to sign with any team they wished—if any teams wanted them.

So, once again, Adam found himself waiting . . .

. . . and hoping.

15

⟨⟨⟨⟨⟨ JOB INTERVIEW ⟩⟩⟩⟩⟩

Players new to the National Football League were called rookies. In early May, they attended rookie camp: three days of practice with the team that chose them. However, the teams didn't have enough rookies to run a full practice. So they also invited 30 to 40 free agents—who were only there to help the rookies get better.

Adam was thrilled to receive a phone call from his favorite team: the Minnesota Vikings! They invited him to try out as one of their extra players. Adam could hardly contain his excitement. He later said, "The little kid inside me went crazy."

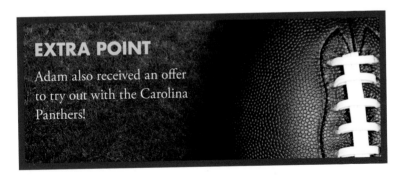

EXTRA POINT

Adam also received an offer to try out with the Carolina Panthers!

Given that Adam was only filling in for a few days, it was a long shot that the team would keep him.

Nevertheless, he had his chance—and that's all that he wanted. However, he also had a promise to keep with Caitlin: to pursue a backup plan.

If football didn't work out, he wasn't sure what his career plans would be. But he needed to earn enough money to live on his own.

Some friends connected him with Patterson Dental, a company that sold dental equipment. The company was in need of an intern, or employee-in-training.

A job interview was scheduled, and Adam dressed in his best suit and tie. The interview seemed mostly typical. The 22-year-old was asked all sorts of questions, and he felt pretty good about his answers.

Eventually, the interviewer asked, "If you could have any job in the world, what would it be?"

Adam thought about saying, "A dental equipment salesman," but both of them would know it was a lie. He decided to be honest, as crazy as the truth might sound to a stranger. "To play in the NFL," he answered.

The interviewer's head snapped upward in surprise. The way he looked at him reminded Adam of Caitlin and the conversation they had shared a few months earlier. The look seemed to say, "That's just a dream. It's time to get real."

The rest of the interview came and went. Adam's peculiar answer did no harm because the gentleman offered Adam the position.

"I'd really like to work for you," said Adam. "But I have a tryout this week with the Vikings. If everything goes well and an opportunity pops up, I have to take it."

The interviewer's eyes widened, and his mouth fell open. But he recovered quickly. He congratulated Adam, wished him luck, and asked Adam to keep him updated.

Adam most certainly would. He felt a little less pressure now. It was nice to know that he had a backup job—even if it wasn't his dream job.

EXTRA POINT

Adam recounts this story and more in "Made in Minnesota," an article he wrote for *The Players' Tribune* (www.theplayerstribune.com).

16

◆◆◆ ROOKIE CAMP ◆◆◆

Rookie camp began on Thursday, May 2, in Eden Prairie, Minnesota. It consisted of five practices over the course of three days. Adam was expecting it to be run like a tryout—kind of like the combine—in which players did their best at various tests of skill. But it wasn't like that. It was more like a team practicing for a game. They worked with coaches in small groups and ran plays as a team.

While it wasn't exactly *like* a tryout, it still *was* a tryout. Only five or six players at camp were assured a spot on the Vikings' final roster. Everyone else was fighting for their dreams—just like Adam.

As camp began, the players were separated into groups. Group 1 consisted of the players whom Minnesota drafted—the players most likely to make the team. Group 2 was the batch of undrafted free agents whom the Vikings signed right after the draft ended. Those players had an outside chance of making the team. All the other players—the fill-in players—were put in Group 3. Those were the young men whom the team had no plans to keep. They were more like "practice buddies" for the players Minnesota truly wanted.

Adam was placed in Group 3.

He needed to change their minds about him—to get the coaches thinking of him as a potential keeper. He needed to work harder and perform better than anyone else on the field. To give himself the best chance, he had to play as fast as he could *on* the field and save the thinking for *off* the field. So in the days leading up to rookie camp, he had memorized the entire playbook—the same playbook that other players studied for several months.

After that, all he could do was his best. But he was playing with the most talented and athletic people he had ever shared a field with. He hoped that his best would be good enough.

The coaches did seem to notice him. By the camp's final practice, Adam was in Group 2—and even spent a bit of time with Group 1. He was going up against future NFL players, and he was doing well against them.

Adam felt proud of himself, but he also understood the situation. At this point in the year, the Vikings could only keep 90 players—including those who were on the team last season. Everyone had a pretty good idea of who those 90 players would be—and Adam wasn't one of them.

At the end of rookie camp, he packed his belongings and prepared to go home.

"Thielen, can you come to the office?" one of the coaches said.

Adam followed him in, where a few coaches were waiting. Adam braced himself for the bad news that would end his dream to become a Viking.

"We like what we saw from you," another coach told him. "But our roster is full."

Adam forced a smile and nodded. "I understand."

"Still, you deserve a chance. You really impressed us. We'd like to sign you."

Adam's mind began to race, and so did his heart. He felt such shock and excitement that it took him a moment to understand what was being said.

"We had to cut another wide receiver to make room for you—somebody we already paid a signing bonus. But we couldn't let you go. We had to make room for you. Congratulations."

The coach held out his hand, and Adam shook it.

For Adam, it might have been the best moment of his life to date. All the hard work—the training, the traveling, the combines, the studying—had paid off. He was a Minnesota Viking. It might only last a few months because in August the Vikings would trim their roster down to 53. But that didn't matter right now. Adam had done it!

He called Caitlin and told her the news. Then he went home to celebrate. But not for long. There was still more work to do. Adam had three-and-a-half months to prove that he belonged on the team.

17

CRISIS FINAL ROSTER CRISIS

Adam graduated from MSU on May 11 with a degree in business management. From there, he focused his energy on football. He studied and trained, day after day, all to give himself the best chance to make the team.

Training camp began at the end of July, and Adam found himself back on the MSU football field. This time, though, he wasn't playing for the Mavericks. He was clad in Vikings purple.

Adam made splash plays and great catches from the very first day. Veteran wide receiver Greg Jennings helped the rookie by offering him tips and advice.

Adam learned a lot about being a professional, but nothing could prepare him for the thrill of his first preseason games. He finally got the chance that he missed in high school: to play at the Metrodome. The roar of 60,000 fans was exhilarating.

On August 16, the Vikings hosted the Buffalo Bills in Week 2 of preseason football. Adam added his name to the stat book with six minutes left in the contest. On third down, reserve quarterback McLeod Bethel-Thompson dropped back to pass and hit Adam with a short throw to the right. The play went for 10 yards and gave Minnesota a first down. A few plays later, the Vikings scored a touchdown, but it wasn't enough. They fell, 20–16.

Two games after that, Adam added another reception for 17 yards to his preseason totals. While his receiving numbers weren't great, he hoped that his work ethic and special teams skills would be enough to earn him a spot on the roster.

It was not. The Vikings cut Adam on August 31. But he didn't stay without a job for long. The very next day, Minnesota brought Adam back as a member of their practice squad. It wasn't exactly being on the team, but it was pretty close to it.

Adam spent the entire 2013 season on the practice squad, along with seven other players. He and his squad-mates helped the Vikings prepare for each game. During practice, they competed against Minnesota's active players by pretending to be the other team.

For Adam, it was an opportunity to further improve his skills while sharing the field with such icons as running back Adrian Peterson, defensive end Jared Allen, and linebacker Chad Greenway. Adam knew that practice squad players rarely became successful in the NFL, but his dreams were alive—and he still had an opportunity to fight for them.

When Christmas came, Adam and Caitlin's tradition of ice-skating in Rice Park continued. This year, though, Adam hoped to make the night extra special. As the snow fell around them, the two skated together. "Marry Me" began to play on the speakers, and Adam knew it was time to act.

He dropped down on one knee and reached into his jacket. But as skilled as he was on the field, his hands failed him at that moment. He tried to hold out the tiny box that contained an engagement ring, but he fumbled. The box fell onto the ice and slid toward Caitlin.

Adam's marriage proposal didn't quite go as planned. But Caitlin said, "yes," and the couple became engaged. Adam's childhood friend Janaye Johnson joined in the special evening, too. She photographed the special moment for Adam.

Unfortunately, not everything was as happy in Minnesota. The season was a disappointment for the Vikings and their fans. The team finished with a 5–10–1 record. Minnesota fired its head coach, Leslie Frazier. In his place, they hired a longtime defensive guru from the Cincinnati Bengals, Mike Zimmer.

Adam had a new coach to impress.

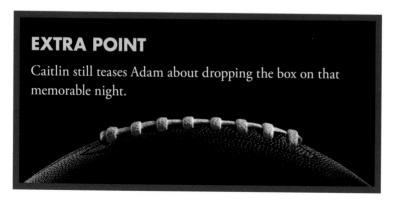

EXTRA POINT

Caitlin still teases Adam about dropping the box on that memorable night.

18

⟨⟨⟨⟨⟨⟨⟩ TOUCHDOWN! ⟨⟨⟨⟨⟨⟨⟩

Adam's hard work throughout the 2013 season had opened a lot of eyes. He had proven that he could perform at a high enough level to compete in the league. On December 30, the Vikings rewarded him with a two-year contract worth nearly $1 million. It seemed that they not only planned to keep him but also intended to make him an active player!

Adam spent the 2014 preseason proving that the Vikings had made a good choice. He performed well enough at wide receiver, but he truly excelled on special teams. Whether it was a key block, a big tackle, or even an explosive return, Adam got himself noticed on kickoffs and punts. He was rewarded with a spot on Minnesota's final 53-man roster.

On September 9, he made his NFL debut in Saint Louis against the Rams. A month later, in Week 5, he caught his first official pass against the Green Bay Packers. It was bittersweet, though. While Adam performed well against a team he grew up rooting against, his Vikings lost in blowout fashion, 42–10.

The crowning moment of Adam's season came in Week 13. It was a frigid Minnesota day, in which the Vikings hosted the Carolina Panthers outdoors at TCF Bank Stadium. Midway through the first quarter, the Panthers lined up to punt at their 42-yard line. Adam stood on the right side of the scrimmage line. When the ball was snapped, he charged straight toward the punter—and no one tried to stop him.

Adam reached out his hands, extended his body, and blocked the punt! As he fell to the ground at the 30-yard line, the ball landed beside him. He grabbed it and hopped off the ground a moment before the punter could reach him. Adam raced to the end zone, scoring his first NFL touchdown and giving the team a 13–0 lead. It was Minnesota's first blocked-punt touchdown in 27 years, and it was a team record for the longest blocked-punt return in history. Minnesota went on to win the game, 31–13, and Adam was awarded the National Football Conference (NFC) Special Teams Player of the Week.

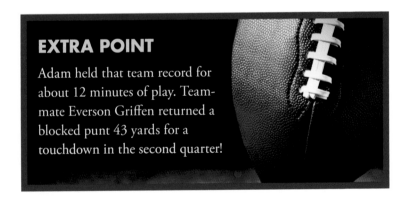

EXTRA POINT

Adam held that team record for about 12 minutes of play. Teammate Everson Griffen returned a blocked punt 43 yards for a touchdown in the second quarter!

Another highlight for Adam came in the final game of the season. He scored his first receiving touchdown on a deep pass from rookie quarterback Teddy Bridgewater. The exciting play went for 44 yards and was the game's only touchdown. It gave Minnesota a third-quarter lead that they would never surrender. After the play, Adam threw the ball to Caitlin, but she missed it. Another fan snagged it, and Caitlin had to ask for it back.

The team won, 13–9, but still finished with a disappointing record of 7–9. There was reason to be optimistic, though. Bridgewater showed promise as Minnesota's quarterback of the future, and Adam had proven to be a valuable asset. He ended the season with 8 catches for 137 yards, as well as 12 tackles on special teams. Perhaps more impressively, he was named to the All-Pro Special Teams Kick Return Unit and was named All-NFC North Special Team Player of the Year by Pro Football Focus. Adam wasn't content, though. He still believed that he could do better.

He trained relentlessly in the offseason. And when he wasn't training, he spent time preparing for a wedding. Adam and Caitlin were married on May 23 during a beautiful church ceremony in the Twin Cities. The bridesmaids wore purple dresses, and the groomsmen donned purple ties.

Adam's nephews, Ethan and Zander, were the ring bearers. They carried in a sign that said, "Uncle Adam,

Adam signed an autograph for his nephew Zander.

here comes the love of your life." After the ceremony, the boys walked out with a sign that read, ". . . and they lived happily ever after with Christ as their center."

It was a wonderful celebration amongst family and friends—and there would be more celebrating to come.

19

⟨⟨⟨⟨⟨ BIG GAMES ⟩⟩⟩⟩⟩

Adam continued his versatile role during the 2015 season. His family saw his skills first-hand when they attended a preseason game on August 15. It was a special trip that celebrated the 88th birthday of Adam's grandpa. Adam delivered a one-of-a-kind gift when he scored a touchdown in the second quarter. The moment was made even more memorable afterward. An excited spectator got the fans in that section to sing "Happy Birthday!"

In the regular season, Adam made play after play on special teams, and he filled in at wide receiver whenever called upon. Week 4 was his best offensive game of the season. He caught 6 passes for 70 yards against the Denver Broncos and helped the Vikings keep the game close. But Denver pulled out a 23–20 victory.

The tight loss against a top team showed that Minnesota could play with anybody. It propelled them on a five-game winning streak.

By Week 17, Minnesota's record stood at a respectable 10–5. They needed just one more win to clinch the NFC North title and a home playoff game. But it wouldn't be easy. The Vikings would be playing in Green Bay against

the Packers—who could also be crowned NFC North champions with a win.

The game proved to be a defensive struggle. Minnesota held the Packers to just one field goal through the first three quarters. In that time, they jumped to a 20–3 lead, thanks to two third-quarter touchdowns. But Green Bay came roaring back in the fourth, scoring 10 straight points.

Down by seven, with time running out, Aaron Rodgers gave his team a chance. But his final pass to the end zone was knocked away by the Vikings.

Adam had a catch for 16 yards in the game. He also carried the ball 2 times for 67 yards, including a 41-yard run on a fake punt. That rushing total was the second highest ever by a Vikings wide receiver in a game!

The win over Green Bay was impressive, but Minnesota had no time to celebrate. They spent the week preparing for their playoff game against Seattle. The Seahawks had crushed the Vikings just a month earlier, 38–7. There was little reason to think this game would be different, but Adam and his teammates were going to give it their best effort. And this time, the Vikings defense came to play.

The game was outdoors, in Minnesota, in January. Everyone expected it to be cold. But the temperature dropped to -6 degrees with a -25-degree wind chill. That made it the coldest game in Vikings history and the third-coldest game in the history of the NFL.

For more than three quarters, the Vikings stifled the Seahawks offense, holding them scoreless. Minnesota,

meanwhile, moved the football just enough to kick three field goals. With 12 minutes left in the game, the Vikings led, 9–0.

The Seattle offense finally struck, thanks to a very strange and lucky play. From the Vikings' 39-yard line, the Seahawks' center snapped the football to star quarterback Russell Wilson. But Wilson wasn't ready for it. The ball sailed past him, all the way back to Seattle's 46-yard line. Wilson fell on the ball, ready to take a 15-yard loss. But the nearest defender was still 10 yards away. So Wilson jumped to his feet, rolled to the right, and threw a pass to a backup receiver that went for 35 yards—all the way to the four-yard line. That set up the Seahawks' first and only touchdown of the game.

Less than four minutes later, Seattle cashed in on a Vikings turnover. They kicked a field goal, giving them a surprising 10–9 lead.

Minnesota still had one scoring drive left in them. They would need it, or their season would be over. With less than two minutes on the clock, Teddy Bridgewater drove his team down the field—eating up yards and time. With only 26 seconds to play, the Vikings set up for an easy game-winning field goal at the nine-yard line.

Minnesota had done it. They had won their playoff game. Players and fans prepared to celebrate one of the team's greatest wins in recent history . . .

. . . until the impossible happened.

The kicker missed the field goal.

Celebration turned to misery. The season was over. The Minnesota Vikings had lost.

EXTRA POINT

A month later, Detroit Lakes held "Adam Thielen Day" on February 7. Adam put on football clinics for local kids, and he was given a key to the city.

20

❮❮❮❮❮ TEAM INJURIES ❯❯❯❯❯

The heartbreaking end to the 2015 season was a tough loss to shake. But it also proved that the Vikings were among the NFL's better teams. The impressive showing against a top-tier opponent left Minnesota with high hopes and lofty goals for the season ahead.

Adam had solidified his spot as an offensive weapon. He was more than a special teams player now. He anticipated seeing plenty of action as a backup wide receiver. And there would be lots of passes to spread around. Quarterback Teddy Bridgewater had improved greatly during the 2015 season—and as the 2016 preseason got underway, he looked even better!

The third-year quarterback was sharp in Minnesota's preseason wins versus the Cincinnati Bengals and San Diego Chargers. Against San Diego, Bridgewater threw for 161 yards in limited action, including a perfect touchdown strike to tight end Kyle Rudolph from 27 yards out.

But a preseason filled with optimism came crashing down on August 30. Bridgewater—who looked poised for a breakout year—suffered a knee injury during practice. The star quarterback's injury was so severe that it immediately became a medical emergency. For a time,

some feared that he might lose his leg. But thanks to the heroic efforts of the Vikings' staff and a team of doctors, Bridgewater's leg was saved. Needless to say, he would miss the entire 2016 season.

The Vikings' team was solid, but they held no hope of contending for the playoffs without a new quarterback. They made the best of a terrible situation by trading two draft picks to the Philadelphia Eagles in exchange for quarterback Sam Bradford. A former number-one pick, Bradford showed signs of promise in his five NFL seasons, but his career had been marred by injuries. The Vikings landed themselves a pretty good player—if they could keep him healthy.

As the season unfolded, Minnesota looked brilliant for making the deal. The Vikings won their first five games.

The streak was even more impressive, considering they lost another key offensive player in Week 2: Adrian Peterson. The star running back injured his knee in a 17–14 win against the Green Bay Packers. He would be out for most—if not all—of the season.

Minnesota's early success was capped by a 31–13 trouncing of the Houston Texans. The win was extra special for Adam. It was his first start of the season, due to a Stefon Diggs injury. It was also the first 100-yard receiving game of Adam's NFL career. On the day, he caught 7 passes for 127 yards, including a 36-yard touchdown.

EXTRA POINT

The performance demonstrated that Adam was good enough to start, and the Vikings noticed. He was propelled into the starting lineup for 8 of Minnesota's final 11 games.

After that impressive beginning to the season, Adam and the Vikings cooled off. The team dropped its next four games before squeaking out a 30–24 win against the Arizona Cardinals. Then the Vikings dropped two more games. After a 5–0 start, Minnesota's record now stood at 6–6. They would need to win at least three of their final four games to have any hope of making the playoffs.

21

~~~~~ TOUGH LOSSES ~~~~~

The Vikings needed to go on a winning streak. Adam did everything he could to ensure that they would. In the very next outing, he sparked the offense with 4 catches for 101 yards, helping Minnesota secure a 25–16 victory against the Jacksonville Jaguars.

A week later, a season of highs and lows swung back down low. In a must-win situation, the Vikings played their worst game of the season. They were blown out at home, 34–6, by a team they were expected to beat: the Indianapolis Colts. Adam suffered a neck injury in the third quarter. He did not return to the game.

The disappointing loss all but eliminated Minnesota from playoff contention. But if they had any hope at all, they would need to win their final two games—no easy feat given that the next matchup was in Green Bay.

Superstar quarterback Aaron Rodgers led the Packers on a long touchdown drive to start the game. Minnesota responded with a successful drive of its own. A beautiful sideline catch by Adam—in which he barely got his toes in bounds—set the Vikings up for a field goal.

Rodgers again marched his team to the end zone, thanks to a couple of long pass plays.

On Minnesota's next possession, Sam Bradford hit Adam with a deep pass down the left sideline. The explosive play went for 33 yards and helped to set up another Vikings field goal.

Rodgers and the Packers' offense could not be stopped, though. The quarterback threw his third touchdown of the half, giving his team a 21–6 lead. Minnesota was in danger of letting the game get away from them. They needed a touchdown—and fast.

From the 29-yard line, Bradford took the snap from center, faked a handoff, and rolled to his right. He saw what he wanted to see and hurled the ball deep downfield. Adam was wide open, streaking toward the end zone. The speedy receiver hauled in the ball at the Packers' 39-yard line and sprinted to the end zone. All together, the play went for 71 yards and kept the Vikings' hopes alive.

Rodgers wasn't going to be outdone. Thanks to a turnover created by a Bradford fumble, he led Green Bay to its fourth touchdown of the half. This time, the quarterback ran the ball in from six yards out. At halftime, the Packers led, 28–13.

Both offenses stalled in the third quarter. Neither team managed to score again until the Packers kicked a field goal to start the fourth. A few minutes later, Rodgers added another touchdown pass to his day, giving Green Bay a 38–13 lead and sealing the Vikings' defeat.

Nevertheless, Adam and his team battled to the end. Adam came up with a few more big catches—and

took a few hard hits in the process. Bradford threw two touchdowns in the game's final minutes. The second was to Adam from eight yards out. Adam jumped high for it in the back of the end zone and landed with both feet in bounds.

The play capped Adam's best receiving day as a pro. He finished with 12 receptions for 202 yards and 2 touchdowns. It was just the fifth 200-yard receiving day in Minnesota Vikings history. That was a small consolation for Adam. His team's playoff hopes were dashed after the 38–25 loss.

Still, there was one more game to be played: at home against the Chicago Bears. Adam needed just 40 yards to finish with 1,000 yards receiving on the season. He didn't get it. In a reversal of the previous game, Adam had a quiet day while the Vikings dominated their opponent. Minnesota won, 38–10, to finish the season at 8–8. Adam caught 1 pass for 7 yards, giving him a total of 69 catches for 967 yards and 5 touchdowns.

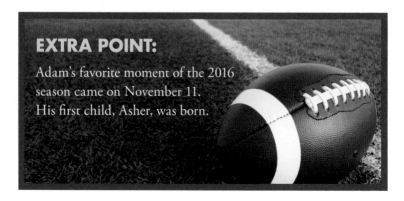

EXTRA POINT:

Adam's favorite moment of the 2016 season came on November 11. His first child, Asher, was born.

22

⟨⟨⟨⟨⟨ KEENUM OR HEINICKE ⟩⟩⟩⟩⟩

In 2016, Adam had proven himself to be a potent offensive weapon. But while Adam was still under contract for the Vikings, he wasn't certain to remain a starter.

Free agency began in March of 2017 for the NFL. Teams could sign players who no longer had contracts with other teams. The Vikings seemed to believe they needed a better wide receiver. They targeted former Chicago Bears star Alshon Jeffery, offering him a contract.

With Stefon Diggs considered the team's top receiver, the addition of Jeffery would most likely reduce Adam's role. Fortunately for Adam—and for the Vikings—Jeffery turned down Minnesota's offer. On March 9, he signed a deal with the Philadelphia Eagles. With that, Adam's job as the Vikings' number-two receiver was secured.

The news got even better for Adam. After missing out on Jeffery, the Vikings extended Adam's contract. They gave him a three-year deal worth as much as $27 million. Adam was locked in to play for his favorite team through the 2020 season.

Minnesota missed out on Jeffery, but they added plenty of other players. Some were expected to be starters—like offensive linemen Mike Remmers and Riley Reiff. Some

Thielen family at a Minnesota Twins game.

free agents, such as running back Latavius Murray and wide receiver Michael Floyd, would see action as backup players. Some, like quarterback Case Keenum and punter Ryan Quigley, were brought in to try and make the team.

The Vikings also made a splash in the second round of the NFL draft. They picked up an explosive running back from Florida State named Dalvin Cook.

The quarterback position was especially tricky for Minnesota. The Vikings knew that Sam Bradford would be their starter. They also had high hopes for the injured Teddy Bridgewater, who might be healthy enough to play by midseason. So it looked as if the Vikings would need a backup quarterback for only the first handful of games.

Keenum was a veteran quarterback who had spent his first four seasons with the Houston Texans and the Saint Louis/Los Angeles Rams. But his play had been inconsistent, so he found himself battling for a job. His competition was Taylor Heinicke, a young player whom the Vikings had been developing since 2015.

Training camp began at the end of July. The Keenum-or-Heinicke question was a debated topic among fans—even though backup quarterbacks didn't usually play much. Would the Vikings be better off with Keenum, an "okay" player who had gameday experience? Or should they go with Heinicke, an unproven talent who was getting better every day?

The first preseason game suggested that Keenum was ahead in the competition. The Vikings traveled to Buffalo to take on the Bills on August 10. Starters like Adam and Sam Bradford didn't play much in the practice game. Keenum got most of the work at quarterback. He performed well, completing 11 of 16 passes for 121 yards.

Yet it was Heinicke who led the Vikings on a scoring drive late in the third quarter. His two-yard touchdown pass to receiver Rodney Adams proved to be the winning score in Minnesota's 17–10 victory.

Keenum again led the Vikings in passing attempts against the Seattle Seahawks. He went 12 for 18 but netted just 70 yards. Heinicke, on the other hand, completed just 6 of 9 passes. But his 84 yards—including a touchdown pass to tight end Bucky Hodges—outshone Keenum's day.

In Minnesota's third preseason contest, Keenum put together his best performance yet. In less than two quarters, he exploded for 139 yards passing and two touchdowns. Again, Heinicke played hero at game's end, running the ball into the end zone on the final play. This two-point conversion gave Minnesota a 32–31 win over the San Francisco 49ers.

Heinicke was performing quite well, but he wasn't playing nearly as much as Keenum. It became clear that Keenum had won the backup quarterback job. Hopefully, the team wouldn't need him. Sam Bradford looked primed for a great year as Minnesota's starting quarterback.

Adam's preseason was quiet. That didn't mean he wasn't ready. Adam hoped to improve upon his numbers from a year ago. His first opportunity would come in a nationally televised matchup against the New Orleans Saints—the first Monday night game of the season.

23

⫷⫷⫷ UP-AND-DOWN START ⫷⫷⫷

Expectations for the Vikings and the Saints were low heading into the season. Each team was projected to win about half its games—or an 8–8 record. Still, both fan bases had high hopes. Minnesota was reputed to have one of the best defenses in the league. New Orleans brought one of the league's best offenses to U.S. Bank Stadium in Minneapolis.

Minnesota fans considered this a "must-win" game— at home against an opponent that went 7–9 the previous year. Fortunately, the Vikings were up to the task.

The Saints opened with a field goal, but the Vikings answered, tying the game late in the first quarter. A second New Orleans field goal gave the visiting team the lead again. But that's when Adam and Sam Bradford went to work.

From the 26-yard line, Bradford connected with Adam on a deep pass that netted 35 yards. The explosive play put the Vikings in range of the end zone. It set up a touchdown pass from Bradford to Stefon Diggs a few plays later, giving Minnesota its first lead of the game, 10–6.

With time winding down in the second quarter, Bradford hit Adam on a similar play. This time, Adam had room to run. He caught the ball 17 yards downfield and streaked ahead, all the way to the 30-yard line before getting tackled. It was a 44-yard gain!

Again, Adam's great play set up a Vikings touchdown, and again the drive was capped by a Bradford-to-Diggs pass, giving the Vikings a 16–6 lead with just 0:03 left in the first half.

The Vikings offense continued to roll in the second half. Adam found openings in the young Saints defense on multiple occasions. Bradford marched his team up and down the field, and Minnesota worked its way to a 26–9 lead in the fourth quarter. The Saints' only touchdown came with under two minutes to go, and the Vikings walked away with an impressive 29–19 victory.

Bradford finished with 346 yards and 3 touchdown passes on his way to being named the NFC Offensive Player of the Week. Adam proved to be Bradford's favorite target, catching 9 passes for 157 yards—one of his best games as a pro.

After their impressive win, the Vikings looked like one of the NFL's top teams. But the news wasn't all good for Minnesota. Quarterback Sam Bradford had hurt his leg during the game. As the Vikings' second game drew near, it was announced that Bradford would not play. Bradford's backup, Case Keenum, was named the starter in Pittsburgh against the Steelers.

Without Bradford, the Vikings became a completely different team. The offense was out of sync all day, and the team managed just nine points. Adam racked up a modest 44 yards receiving as the Vikings were thumped, 26–9.

The team needed Bradford back—and fast. But they weren't going to get him. The star quarterback was ruled out for Week 3, at home against the Tampa Bay Buccaneers—a team that many experts believed would make the playoffs.

Vikings fans began to get nervous. Some members of the local media suggested that a loss might spiral the season out of control. Could Minnesota lose five or six games in a row? Without Sam Bradford, it certainly looked possible.

The fate of the entire season seemed to hinge on Keenum's performance. As his team took the field on Sunday, September 24, no one knew what to expect.

The veteran quarterback got the Vikings started early. He connected with Adam on a deep pass down the left side of the field. The play went for 45 yards and led to a touchdown run by rookie standout Dalvin Cook.

In the second quarter, Keenum kept the offense moving. He fired touchdown passes to Jarius Wright and Stefon Diggs. The Vikings led 21–3 at halftime.

A 59-yard touchdown pass to Diggs in the third quarter all but sealed the victory. Minnesota rolled to a 34–17 win. Adam put together a solid game, catching 5 passes for 98 yards. But Keenum was the star on this day. He completed 25 of 33 passes, throwing for 369 yards and 3 touchdowns. The win put the Vikings' record at 2–1.

In Week 4, though, the inconsistent offense was cold again. The defense did its best to carry the team, holding the Detroit Lions to 14 points. But the offense managed just 7 points. On top of that, the team lost its star running back, Dalvin Cook, to a knee injury. He would not play again for the rest of the season.

EXTRA POINT:

In 2017, Randy Moss interviewed Adam on ESPN. They joked about how they had met at training camp 14 years earlier.

24

EMOTIONAL SEASON

Going into Week 5, there was more bad news: Minnesota would be playing in Chicago. Since 2001, the Vikings had won just 2 of 16 games on the road against the Bears. But Chicago ranked among the league's bottom teams this year. Plus, Minnesota's offense would be getting a big boost: Bradford was back! He was named the Vikings' starter for this important divisional game.

If fans thought the Vikings would roll to an easy win, they were wrong. From the beginning, Bradford looked off. The Vikings offense sputtered. They even gave up a two-point safety late in the first quarter, when Bradford was sacked in the end zone. Minnesota's defense, however, dominated the first half. They created a turnover that led to a field goal near the end of the second quarter. At halftime, the Vikings led, 3–2.

Bradford's return came to an early end, with his leg still bothering him and with the offense unable to score. Keenum was called upon to take Bradford's place. The backup quarterback sparked two touchdowns in the third quarter—but the Bears answered each time. A sneaky fake punt and a fluky tipped-pass had the Bears and Vikings tied 17–17 in the fourth quarter.

Adam with his son, Asher, at a football game.

Minnesota's defense again responded. They intercepted a pass that put the team in field goal position. The Vikings ran the game clock down to 16 seconds before kicking the game-winning field goal.

The victory put Minnesota at 3–2, and it solidified Keenum's role as starting QB for at least the next few games. But if Bradford became healthy—or if Keenum faltered—he would find himself on the bench again.

While Minnesota's quarterback position remained a question, Adam's importance to the team did not. Five weeks in, Adam was averaging 6 catches and 78 yards per game. He didn't have a touchdown yet, but he and fellow wide receiver Stefon Diggs were the Vikings' key players on offense—especially with injuries to Bradford and Dalvin Cook.

Adam and Diggs were regarded by many as the best wide receiver duo in the league. But Diggs was dinged up, too. He could not contribute to the Vikings' next two games, victories against both Green Bay (24–10) and Baltimore (24–16).

Diggs returned to action versus the Cleveland Browns in Week 8—a game played in London, England. Adam scored his first touchdown of the season on an 18-yard pass from Keenum. Despite trailing late in the third quarter, the Vikings recorded the game's final 18 points and won, 33–16.

Keenum had led the Vikings to four straight wins, but questions still swirled around him. How long could he keep winning? What would happen when Bradford came back? What if Teddy Bridgewater was well enough to play? Would Minnesota keep Bradford, Bridgewater, and Keenum on the roster—or would one of them, most likely Keenum, get cut from the team?

Slowly, week by week, Keenum put those questions to rest. With Adam positioned as his favorite target, Keenum entered a stretch of games in which he was arguably the best quarterback in the NFL. Minnesota won their next four games. In those victories, Keenum averaged 273 yards

passing per game, threw 9 touchdown passes, and ran for a touchdown, too.

At the same time, Adam proved himself as one of the top receivers in the game. Between weeks 10 and 13, he caught 26 passes for 429 yards and scored two more times. His impressive string of games was highlighted by a 38–30 victory against Washington. Adam caught 8 passes and went for a season-high 166 yards receiving. That included a 7-yard touchdown catch.

EXTRA POINT

In Week 12, Adam racked up 89 yards receiving in Detroit. It gave him 1,005 yards on the season, making him Minnesota's first 1,000-yard receiver in 8 years!

Week 14 found the Vikings playing against the Carolina Panthers. Adam once again went for more than 100 yards receiving, but this time, it wasn't enough. Minnesota's eight-game winning streak came to an end as the team fell, 31–24.

Still, the Vikings' record stood at 10–3. They were one of the league's best teams, and they were primed for a successful playoff push. Keenum's role as starting quarterback was no longer in question. He had earned the right to play out the rest of the season. Everything seemed to be going Minnesota's way. And the best news of all . . . after more than a year of rehabilitation, Teddy Bridgewater was okayed to play. He would be active for the game against Cincinnati, suiting up as Keenum's backup.

Minnesota was a great team. They were playing at home in front of a frenzied crowd of fans. The Vikings were already favored to win. But the news of Bridgewater's return was like an electrical charge that amped up the team—and the entire state.

The Bengals never stood a chance.

The Vikings scored the first 34 points of the game. And with the victory assured, Bridgewater got his chance to play. The stadium erupted into cheers as the beloved young quarterback took the field in the fourth quarter. His only pass attempt was an interception, but that didn't matter. In a regular season filled with spectacular plays and amazing victories, Bridgewater's return to action topped them all. Nothing could feel as powerful or more memorable than seeing Bridgewater back on the field, standing with his teammates.

At least, that's what the Vikings' faithful fans believed, until . . .

25

MINNEAPOLIS MIRACLE

The Vikings closed out the season with two more wins, giving them a record of 13–3. That was good enough to earn a number-two seed in the National Football Conference (NFC) playoffs. Adam ended up with 91 receptions, 1,276 yards, and 4 touchdowns. The Vikings got a bye in the first round and a home game in the second round—a rematch against the New Orleans Saints.

Both teams were very different than they had been in Week 1 of the season. The Vikings were starting a different quarterback. The Saints had seen the emergence of their rookie running back, Alvin Kamara. Plus, their defense had improved greatly. And they were still led by star quarterback Drew Brees. All told, New Orleans had finished with an impressive 11–5 record.

Most experts predicted a close, hard-fought game that either team could win. But as the first half unfolded, it looked like those experts were wrong. The Vikings' offense easily drove down the field for a touchdown on their first possession. And they kept going, racking up 17 points in the first half.

For as good as the offense looked, the defense played even better. New Orleans didn't convert a single third down. Brees threw two interceptions and was sacked twice as his team was shut out.

The 17–0 halftime score suggested that this game would be a laugher. But the second half was a different story. Brees and the Saints reeled off two touchdowns, cutting the score to 17–14.

Minnesota added a field goal with 10 minutes left in the game. But a blocked punt set up New Orleans for their third touchdown of the half—and their first lead of the game, 21–20. Minnesota had just 3:01 left to score, or their season would be over.

It was crunch time, and Keenum knew what to do. He went to his best receiver, lofting a pass to Adam 20 yards downfield. Adam jumped as high as he could and extended his yellow gloves as far as he could reach. He pulled the ball into his body and rolled down at the 41-yard line. The 23-yard play set Minnesota up nicely. A few quick plays and a few yards later, Vikings kicker Kai Forbath drilled a field goal that put his team ahead, 23–21 with just 1:29 on the clock. Minnesota was going to win!

But Drew Brees had something to say about that. In a minute, he drove his team all the way to the Vikings' 25-yard line. The Saints kicked a field goal of their own, giving them a 24–23 lead—and almost certain victory with just 25 seconds left.

It would take a miracle for Minnesota to win.

The Vikings' offense began at their own 20-yard line. Keenum quickly completed a pass to Stefon Diggs for

19 yards, and the team called their final timeout to stop the clock.

They needed about 25 or 30 yards for a chance at another field goal, and they only had seconds to get it. The bigger problem, though, was that they no longer had any timeouts. So if anyone got tackled in bounds, the game would be over. Keenum had to complete a deep pass to a receiver, and then the receiver had to get out of bounds to stop the clock. Meanwhile, the Saints were guarding the sidelines, trying not to let the receivers run out of bounds.

With just 10 seconds to go, there was little hope. But Adam and his team weren't about to give up. Keenum called a play that would have his receivers spread out along both sidelines. When the ball was snapped, his receivers took off. Adam streaked down the left side of the field and

Diggs down the right. Keenum looked for Adam, wanting to get him the ball, but Adam was well covered. So Keenum looked right. Time was running out; he couldn't wait. The quarterback shuffled forward a few steps and heaved the ball deep down the right sideline.

The ball traveled 27 yards in the air, and the throw was high. Suddenly, Diggs stopped and jumped. In one quick motion, his hands snapped into the air and snagged the ball at the Saints' 35-yard line. The pass was complete!

There were still five seconds. If Diggs stepped out of bounds, Minnesota would have a chance at a long field goal. But Diggs didn't run out of bounds. The Saints defender had tried to tackle Diggs and missed. There was no one between the receiver and the end zone.

So he ran.

He didn't stop until he reached the end zone. Touchdown! With no time left on the clock, Minnesota had just defeated the Saints, 29–24, on one of the most amazing plays in NFL history.

26

CRGCCB PRO BOWL ACGCCBD

The win against New Orleans was thrilling, but it was also emotionally draining. A week later, the Vikings played flat in the NFC Championship. They lost to the Philadelphia Eagles, 38–7, ending a magical season.

But Adam had another game to play. NFL fans, players, and coaches had recognized his tremendous year. They voted him into the Pro Bowl, an exhibition game that featured the very best players from across the league. Adam was set to join the NFC against the American Football Conference (AFC).

Adam flew to Orlando, Florida, to take part in a variety of activities throughout the week. The NFL kept fans entertained and players busy with such events as flag football, skills challenges, and youth football clinics, not to mention team practices leading up to the game.

On Sunday, January 28, 2018, the stage was set at Orlando's Camping World Stadium for the fun-spirited contest. The Pro Bowl was always special to players and to fans, as bitter rivals became teammates and friends. Adam found himself playing on the same side as such divisional foes as Davante Adams (Green Bay Packers) and Darius Slay (Detroit Lions).

The football game began mid-afternoon. Adam's NFC squad, wearing blue jerseys, lined up with the ball at the 25-yard line. The team of all-stars were led by New Orleans Saints quarterback Drew Brees, who sparked a 75-yard march toward the end zone.

Brees passed the NFC most of the way there. He connected with a variety of receivers on that initial drive: Michael Thomas (Saints), Doug Baldwin (Seattle Seahawks), Todd Gurley (Los Angeles Rams), Adam's teammate Kyle Rudolph, and others. But Adam was the focal point. His number 19 was first called with the NFC at their 49-yard line. He lined up in the slot position on the right side of the field.

As the center snapped the football to Brees, Adam darted toward the middle of the field. The linebackers for the AFC dropped back into coverage, and Adam found an empty area in front of them. He was wide open.

Brees, one of the best quarterbacks ever to play the game, didn't waste a moment. He zipped the ball to Adam, who raced toward the left sideline. Adam caught the ball, spun forward, and was tackled by another all-time great: Baltimore Ravens linebacker Terrell Suggs.

For the young wide receiver from a small town in rural Minnesota, another dream had come true. Adam had just made his mark in the Pro Bowl. He was on the field. He was competing with and against the top players in the NFL. He had come so far, and he had accomplished so much. But he wasn't finished.

Adam played catch with his son, Asher, at a Pro Bowl event.

Brees completed two passes to Rudolph, bringing the NFC down to the 8-yard line. A new play was called in the huddle, and Adam lined up as the wide receiver on the left side of the field. He was alone out there, one on one against Jacksonville Jaguars cornerback A.J. Bouye. The ball was snapped, and Adam raced forward. After three steps, he cut sharply to his right and angled his route toward the end zone.

Again, Brees didn't hesitate. He hurled the football toward Adam and put it right in the receiver's stomach. Adam clutched the ball, ducked low, and rolled toward the goal line as Bouye tackled him.

Touchdown!

Adam had given the NFC a 6–0 lead. He celebrated with Baldwin, Gurley, Brees, and more of his new teammates. It was a perfect moment and a fitting end to a dream season for Adam.

The Pro Bowl receiver didn't see as much action over the remainder of the game. He finished with 3 catches for 25 yards. Unfortunately, Adam's NFC team lost, 24–23, thanks to an AFC touchdown in the final two minutes of the game. But the outcome didn't diminish Adam's glorious day. After years of hard work, dedication, and perseverance, he had become one of the best wide receivers in the NFL.

The end of the 2017–2018 football year brought time for Adam to rest and recover from a hard-fought season. But he didn't rest for long. Adam knew that the next season would come soon enough. He needed to work and work and work to become even better.

Guided by his faith and a winning attitude, Adam believed that he could help the Vikings continue their winning ways—maybe even bring a National Football League championship to Minnesota.

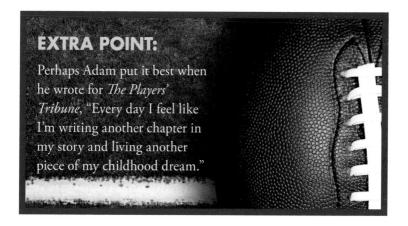

EXTRA POINT:

Perhaps Adam put it best when he wrote for *The Players' Tribune*, "Every day I feel like I'm writing another chapter in my story and living another piece of my childhood dream."

EPILOGUE

Adam has enjoyed great success on the football field, and it's no secret how he's gotten there. He found something that he was passionate about. He devoted himself to it. He practiced as hard and as often as he could. He never stopped believing that he could get better. And he never gave in. The authors hope that Adam's story inspires you to find your passion and to chase your dreams.

During the offseason, Adam and Caitlin stay active with charities that benefit others. Adam's past efforts have included fundraisers, charity golf tournaments, Christmas donations, and more.

In 2018, Adam and Caitlin launched their own charity, the Thielen Foundation. Its mission is "to serve, educate and inspire people to reach their full potential."

Adam and his new foundation went to work quickly, hosting their first event on June 24: a youth football camp. Adam worked with elementary-school-aged to high-school-aged students. He spent the day teaching them about achieving success in football and in life.

For more information about the Thielen Foundation, visit thielenfoundation.org.

ON THE INTERNET

Sports articles about Adam's high school games:
www.DL-Online.com

Photo shoots in the Twin Cities area:
www.JanayeJohnsonPhotography.com

Photo shoots in the Detroit Lakes area:
www.CaulfieldStudios.com

Back to Pass
Goal-Minded
Out at Home
Save the Season!

Read the fast-paced, action-packed stories. Make the right choices. Find your way to the "winning" ending!

SOURCES

Breech, John. "Teddy Bridgewater Put on PUP List, Explains How Close He Was to Losing His Leg." CBS Sports (cbssports.com). July 27, 2017.

Brinson, Will. CBS Sports (cbssports.com).
- "2017 NFL Season Win Total Over/Under Picks for NFC South." May 12, 2017.
- "2017 NFL Season Win Total Over/Under Picks for NFC North." May 11, 2017.

Coller, Matthew. "How Basketball Helped Shape Adam Thielen's NFL Career." 1500 ESPN Twin Cities (1500espn.com). October 14, 2017.

DL News Staff. DL-Online (dl-online.com).
- "Metro All-Stars Squeak One Past Outstate." July 2, 2008.
- "Lakers Are Class 2A State Golfing Co-Champions." June 10, 2008.
- "Strong Finish and Broken Records Highlight DL's Season." March 19, 2008.
- "Thielen Becomes Most Prolific Scorer in DL Boys' Basketball History." February 27, 2008.
- "Elite Company." January 26, 2008.
- "DL's Thielen Scores Career Point 1,000." January 23, 2008.
- "Thielen Propels Laker Boy Cagers to First Win." December 19, 2007.
- "Plenty of Accolades Come out of 2007 Laker Football Season: DL Dominates Opponents for Perfect Season; Earns Trip to Section Championship." November 11, 2007.
- "Sartell Upstages Lakers in Section 8-4A Championship." November 3, 2007.
- "No Playoff Surprises This Time for Lakers." October 24, 2007.
- "Lakers Win Battle of North Country Conference Powers." October 13, 2007.
- "Lakers Cash in Turnovers for 47–20 Victory." September 1, 2007.
- "Shooting Woes Plague DL Boys' Basketball." March 21, 2007.
- "Thomsen and Thielen Return to Lead DL Boy Cagers." November 29, 2006.
- "Year 2006 Was an Introduction of Things to Come for Lakers." November 9, 2006.

Escalante, Angela (Summer 2018). Interviews.

ESPN: The Worldwide Leader in Sports (espn.com)
- "Adam Thielen." Accessed July 2018.
- "Minnesota Vikings NFL." Accessed July 2018.
- "Vikings vs. Cowboys – November 26, 1998." Accessed July 2018.

Forgrave, Reid. "Adam Thielen: The Vikings' Unlikely Star." *Minnesota Monthly* (minnesotamonthly.com). August 18, 2017.

Glover, Ted. "Sam Bradford Wins NFC Offensive Player of the Week." Daily Norseman (dailynorseman.com). September 13, 2017.

Goessling, Ben. "Sam Bradford 'Excited for a New Chapter' after Trade to Vikings." ESPN: The Worldwide Leader in Sports (espn.com). September 4, 2016.

Johnson, Janaye (Summer 2018). Interviews.

Krammer, Andrew. "Receiver Adam Thielen Moves into the Vikings' 1,000-yard Club — the First Since Sidney Rice in 2009." *Star Tribune* (startribune.com). November 23, 2017.

McGuinness, Gordon. "2014 PFF All-Pro Special Teams." Pro Football Focus (profootballfocus.com). January 6, 2015.

Minnesota State University, Mankato Athletics. The Official Website of the Minnesota State Mavericks (msumavericks.com).
- "Adam Thielen." Accessed July 2018.
- Valdosta State vs. Minnesota State. December 8, 2012.
- Southwest Minnesota State vs. Minnesota State. October 13, 2012.
- Wayne State vs. Minnesota State. October 22, 2011.
- Northern State vs. Minnesota State. September 11, 2010.

Mountford, Michael. "2014 PFF All-NFC North Team." Pro Football Focus (profootballfocus.com). January 21, 2015.

Murphy, Chris. "'He Always Had a Plan': The Unlikely Rise to NFL Stardom for Detroit Lakes' Adam Thielen." *Duluth News Tribune* (duluthnewstribune.com). December 23, 2017.

"NFL 2013 Draft." NFL.com (nfl.com). Accessed July 2018.

NFL Countdown. "Adam Thielen's Unorthodox Journey to the NFL." ESPN (espn.com). December 3 ,2017.

"NFL Game Center." NFL.com (nfl.com).
- 2018 Pro Bowl. January 28, 2018.
- New Orleans vs. Minnesota. January 14, 2018.
- Cincinnati vs. Minnesota. December 17, 2017.
- Cleveland vs. Minnesota. October 29, 2017.
- Chicago vs. Minnesota. October 9, 2017.
- Tampa Bay vs. Minnesota. September 24, 2017.
- New Orleans vs. Minnesota. September 11, 2017.
- Seattle vs. Minnesota. August 18, 2017.
- Buffalo vs. Minnesota. August 10, 2017.
- Green Bay vs. Minnesota. December 24, 2016.
- Indianapolis vs. Minnesota. December 18, 2016.
- San Diego vs. Minnesota. August 28, 2016.
- Seattle vs. Minnesota. January 10, 2016.
- Green Bay vs. Minnesota. January 3, 2016.
- Tampa Bay vs. Minnesota. August 15, 2015.
- Chicago vs. Minnesota. December 28, 2014.
- Carolina vs. Minnesota. November 30, 2014.
- Tennessee vs. Minnesota. August 29, 2013.
- Buffalo vs. Minnesota. August 16, 2013.

Patra, Kevin. "Alshon Jeffery, Eagles Agree to One-Year Deal." NFL.com (nfl.com). March 10, 2017.

"Probability of Competing Beyond High School." NCAA (ncaa.org). Accessed July 2018.

Spotrac (spotrac.com).
- "Minnesota Vikings 2015 Salary Cap." Accessed July 2018.
- "Minnesota Vikings 2014 Salary Cap." Accessed July 2018.

Thielen, Adam. "Made in Minnesota." *The Players' Tribune* (theplayerstribune.com). October 12, 2017.

Thielen, Caitlin (Summer 2018). Interviews.

Thielen, Jayne (Summer 2018). Interviews.

Thielen, Peter. (Summer 2018). Interviews.

Thielen Foundation. "Adam Thielen's Inaugural Youth Football Camp" (thielenfoundation.org). June 24, 2018.

Tomasson, Chris. *Pioneer Press* (twincities.com).
- "Vikings Sending Everson Griffen, Anthony Barr, Xavier Rhodes, Adam Thielen to Pro Bowl." December 19, 2017.
- "Vikings, WR Adam Thielen Reach Agreement on Contract." March 16, 2017.

VonRuden, Mary (Summer 2018). Interviews.

Welken, Amanda (Summer 2018). Interviews.

Wierima, Brian. DL-Online (dl-online.com).
- "Thielen Making Strides at Vikings' Training Camp." July 31, 2013.
- "Vikings Training Camp: A Budding NFL Career Potentially Starting for Thielen." July 24, 2013.
- "Thielen Officially Signs with Minnesota Vikings." May 7, 2013.

Williams, Robert. "Detroit Lakes Celebrates 'Adam Thielen Day' with Events That Allow the Viking to Give Back to His Hometown." *Grand Forks Herald* (grandforksherald.com). February 8, 2015.

PHOTOGRAPHY CREDITS

ABOUT THE AUTHORS

Lindsay VonRuden grew up in Detroit Lakes, Minnesota. She loved writing stories and pretending to teach as a young girl. Fittingly enough, she is now an elementary teacher and a budding author. When Lindsay isn't teaching, she prefers to spend her time outdoors with family, friends, and her beloved dog, Remy. She believes that the best way to live life is as a never-ending adventure. She has created a life list of accomplishments she'd like to complete. So far, Lindsay has checked off some exhilarating challenges, such as shark cage diving, bungee jumping, zorbing, glowworm cave rafting, and, now, writing a book!

Ryan Jacobson is an author and presenter. He prides himself on writing high-interest books for children of all ages, so he can talk picture books in kindergarten, ghost stories in high school, and other fun stuff in between. He lives in rural Minnesota and has been a lifelong Minnesota sports fan.